# THE VALUE OF COMPASSION

## The Story of Florence Nightingale

**VALUE** COMMUNICATIONS, INC.
PUBLISHERS
SAN DIEGO, CALIFORNIA

# THE VALUE OF COMPASSION

The Story of

Florence Nightingale

BY ANN DONEGAN JOHNSON

First Edition
Manufactured in the United States of America.
For information write to: ValueTales,
9601 Arrow Drive, San Diego, CA 92123

*All dialogue in the text is fictitious.*

Library of Congress Catalog Card Number 86-210004

ISBN 0-86679-041-1

This tale is about Florence Nightingale,
the compassionate woman who is
widely known as the founder of
modern nursing. The story that follows
is based on events in her life. More
historical facts about Florence
Nightingale can be found on page 63.

# Once upon a time...

in far-off Italy, a young English couple were admiring their brand-new baby daughter.

"Isn't she lovely?" Mrs. Nightingale said.

"She is indeed," agreed Mr. Nightingale. "What shall we name her?"

"Well, it occurred to me, why not call her Florence?" Florence was the name of the city in Italy where their little girl was born.

"A splendid idea!" cried her husband. "Yes, Florence Nightingale sounds just right for her."

One evening when Florence was almost a year old and her sister, Parthenope, was two, Mrs. Nightingale spoke thoughtfully to her husband.

"I think we should go back to England," she said. By now the Nightingales had been living in Italy for three years.

"Aren't you happy here?" asked Mr. Nightingale.

"Yes, of course," replied his wife. "It's been wonderful. But the girls are growing so fast. We must think of them—and their future."

"You're right," agreed Mr. Nightingale. "It is time we established ourselves in our own country."

And so the Nightingales packed up all their trunks and returned to their country estate in Derbyshire, England. It was called Lea Hurst, and Mr. Nightingale had had a fine new house built there for his family.

"It's delightful!" exclaimed Mrs. Nightingale when she saw it. "And such a wonderful view! I shall be able to invite all my friends to visit and have marvellous parties."

Mrs. Nightingale loved to have lots of people around.

As Florence and Parthenope were growing up, the house was always full of friends and relatives. They enjoyed the company, and Florence was especially happy when there were small children among the visitors.

"Do let me take care of the little ones," she would beg. Then she would spend all her time looking after them— inventing games to amuse them and making sure they didn't hurt themselves.

Among the children brought to visit the Nightingales, Florence had a particular favorite—a little cousin named Robert.

"Poor wee thing," said Florence to her sister as she bounced Robert on her knee. "Hardly anyone pays any attention to him, except maybe to say what an ugly baby he is."

"Well," observed Parthenope, "it's true isn't it?"

"But that's no reason to love him less," protested Florence.

You see, Florence was a very compassionate little girl. She could never see misfortune without feeling great pity and wanting desperately to do something about it.

It was the same with animals. If Florence heard that a horse was injured or a calf was sickly, she haunted the stable or barn doing whatever she could to help. And she was forever rescuing orphaned squirrels or wounded birds and caring for them until they could manage on their own.

"I declare," said Mr. Nightingale one day when he came upon Florence and one of her special patients. "I think you worry more about that sparrow than you do about your family."

"But, Father," Florence pointed out, "there's no need for me to worry about any of you. You are all strong and healthy."

"Yes, of course," laughed her father. "Just don't let your compassionate heart make you neglect your lessons."

Mr. Nightingale himself looked after his daughters' education. He taught them Latin, Greek, French, Italian, history, philosophy and mathematics.

Florence was a keen student, but Parthenope did not much enjoy the lessons. "I just don't see why we need to know all this," she grumbled. "I'd much rather be helping Mother arrange the flowers for the party tonight."

Florence simply couldn't understand it. She found arranging flowers *very* boring.

When the girls were not busy studying, they often accompanied their mother on her weekly visit to the cottages around Lea Hurst. Many poor people lived in these cottages, and Mrs. Nightingale took them food and other necessities.

"It is our duty to help those less fortunate than ourselves," she would tell her daughters.

Florence did not need to be told. Her compassionate young heart ached to see the misery in which some of the cottagers lived. "It just isn't fair that these people are so poor!" she cried.

"I know," replied her mother. "But we do what we can for them, and we can't change the world."

But Florence felt that she could be doing more for the cottagers. As she grew older, she began visiting them on her own, especially those who were sick. She would tidy their rooms, rub their backs, make them tea or broth and then sit quietly and talk to them for a while.

"Where's Florence?" asked Mr. Nightingale as he sat down to dinner one evening when Florence was sixteen.

Before anyone could answer, Florence herself came flying into the dining-room. "I'm sorry I'm late. Old Granny Clarkson is very ill and she likes to have me sit with her."

"That's the third time this week, Florence," scolded her mother. "Compassion is all very well, but it can be carried too far. You have other obligations."

"I know I do, but it seems so little to do if it comforts her . . ."

"Well, make sure you are on time tomorrow. We are having guests."

"Oh, not again," thought Florence. For some time now she had been finding her mother's parties more and more pointless and tiresome.

"Do stop moping, Florence, and come and greet our guests," urged Mrs. Nightingale as the first carriage pulled up to the door. "What's wrong with you anyway?"

"It's just that it all seems like such a waste of time," murmured her daughter.

"Nonsense," replied Mrs. Nightingale. "With all those nice young men who think the world of you! What more could a girl your age want? Now do stop being so critical and try to enjoy yourself like other young people."

"Come on, Florence," said Parthenope. "The music and dancing will be so much fun and the boys are so handsome."

Florence sighed. "There has to be more to life than these silly parties," she said to herself. But being a polite and considerate person, she went and greeted the guests with a smile.

"Dear me, thank goodness that's over!" thought Florence as she snuggled into her bed. "I'm not sure I can take many more evenings like that."

"Oh, stop feeling sorry for yourself Florence Nightingale," scolded a little voice.

Florence sat bolt upright. "Who's there?" she cried.

"Just me," answered the voice.

Florence looked around. The voice seemed to come from the lamp beside her bed. "But lamps don't speak," she quavered.

"Maybe they do, maybe they don't," replied the lamp. "How can you be so sure?"

"Who are you?" demanded Florence.

"A friend. You may call me what you like."

Florence thought for a moment. "I know, I shall call you Lucy. It means 'light,' so it's a perfect name for a lamp. But what are you doing here, Lucy?"

"Well, you don't seem to be very happy with your life, and I thought you could use someone to talk to."

Now Florence *was* sure that lamps don't speak, but she realized that she was imagining Lucy because she did indeed need someone to talk to. "You were right," she admitted.

"I usually am," said Lucy airily. "Now then, what are you going to do about your life?"

"That's just the trouble," wailed Florence. "I don't know what to do—I feel so useless."

"You help your mother, don't you?" suggested Lucy.

"I sort and count linens and china and silver, if that's what you mean. It just makes things worse. How can reasonable people want all that stuff when so many others live in such misery?"

"I see your point," agreed Lucy.

"But do you see what I can do about it?"

"That's something you will have to decide for yourself. You're a very compassionate person, but you're still quite young. My advice is to keep looking around you to see what needs to be done. In time you will think of ways to help people."

"I do hope you're right," sighed Florence.

Twice every year the Nightingales spent several weeks in London. These times were particularly difficult for Florence. She was not allowed to wander around alone the way she could at Lea Hurst, and so there seemed to be no way for her to do anything for those in need of help.

"Did you see those children, Parthenope, as we drove into town?" she said to her sister. "They looked so sickly and hungry and cold. Did you see the filth and garbage in the streets—running down into the river that people get their drinking water from?"

"Of course I saw, Florence. But what point is there in thinking about such unpleasant things?"

"I can't help it," cried Florence. "Those people are no different from us except that they have no money. They shouldn't have to live in such conditions."

"I agree," replied Parthenope, "but there really isn't much we can do for them."

"Nonsense!" said a little voice sternly. "I hope I never hear you talk like that, Florence. There is a lot a person with compassion and determination can do."

"Oh Lucy," whispered Florence, "I am so glad you're here!" She glanced anxiously at Parthenope, wondering what her sister might make of a talking lamp. But Florence was the only one who could see and hear her little friend.

The days seemed an endless string of parties and gossipy visits and preparations for more parties. Florence became very depressed.

"Oh, do snap out of your bad mood," said her mother impatiently. "All you do is sit there and mope. Why can't you be like your sister and enjoy the nice young people around you?"

But Florence had no interest in the social whirl. She tried to explain to her mother that she needed to be doing something more worthwhile, but it did no good.

"What am I going to do, Lucy?" Florence whispered wearily to her friend.

"Don't get too down-hearted," answered Lucy. "You will know when the time comes."

"I am worried about Florence," said Mrs. Nightingale to her husband as their stay in London neared its end. "She seems to have no interest in anything."

"I don't think that's completely true," replied Florence's father. "She is a good student and enjoys learning."

"Yes, but a girl her age should be wanting to have fun too. Why don't we take her on a trip? We could go back to Italy. Maybe that will help change her ideas."

Mr. Nightingale thought for a while. "That is a very good suggestion."

And so the Nightingales set out for Italy. They crossed France in a large coach that Mr. Nightingale had designed himself. They had six attendants and the coach was drawn by three pairs of horses.

Florence kept careful notes on all the places they passed through—notes about distances and the weather and laws and the conditions in which people lived. She also enjoyed herself enormously. She loved the beautiful cathedrals and the squares and palaces they saw and the wonderful concerts they heard.

Best of all, she loved the city of Florence, where they went to splendid balls and met many very interesting people.

Eventually it was time to go back to England.
Mrs. Nightingale was delighted with the way her idea had turned out. At last Florence seemed to be behaving like other girls her age.

But Florence had not really forgotten her concern for the poor and helpless of the world.

As soon as she got back to Lea Hurst, Florence started visiting the sick people in the village again. In the evening she would sit and talk quietly to Lucy about their problems.

"I can give them compassion, Lucy, and maybe make them a bit more comfortable, but that's not enough. I don't know what to do to make them *well*. If only I knew more!"

"Can't you learn?" asked Lucy.

And suddenly it came to Florence. She knew what she wanted to do.

"That's it, Lucy!" she exclaimed. "I will learn. I'll learn everything I can about hospitals and about diseases and injuries and how to treat each one. I am going to become a nurse!"

"Oh dear," said Lucy, "what on earth will your family say?"

Florence's family was shocked. At that time, nursing was not a respected profession.

"A daughter of mine doing nursing—never!" cried her horrified mother.

"Florence, you just can't be a nurse," shrieked her sister. "What would people say?"

"Girls of your background don't do nursing," added her father more gently. "The conditions are appalling. You would not be able to stand it."

Mrs. Nightingale and Parthenope became quite upset at the thought of it all. Argument followed argument. Months passed—and years.

But Florence was determined.

She bought books on medicine and studied them in her room at night. She had her friends on the continent send her reports on hospitals and institutions for the poor in other countries.

"What is all that for?" asked Lucy, eyeing the mountains of paper surrounding Florence.

"Well, I have to know what is going on before I can do anything about it," Florence explained.

"I can't argue with that," said her friend.

One day, Florence even persuaded a doctor friend of her father's to show her around a London hospital. She was horrified at what she saw.

The conditions were dreadful. The patients were dirty and uncared for. The wards and beds were filthy, with rats running across the floor. There were not enough doctors to take care of everyone. The nurses and attendants were almost as dirty as the patients.

"I can understand why your parents are so set against your nursing," said Lucy.

"I am going to change all this," vowed Florence. She was more determined than ever to fulfill her dream of becoming a nurse and making nursing a respectable job.

Florence knew she still had much more to learn about nursing.

"I believe they are making great improvements in hospitals in other countries," said Lucy one day. "Why don't you accept some of those invitations from friends who want you to visit them abroad? You might be able to visit some hospitals while you are at it and study how they are run."

"Lucy, what a splendid idea!" cried Florence. "And if I just don't mention hospitals to Mother, she won't even worry about me." Indeed, Mrs. Nightingale, remembering how well the earlier trip had worked to distract Florence, was quite happy to send her daughter off on a new round of visits.

Florence traveled around France and Germany and Ireland. Everywhere she went she visited hospitals and learned everything she could about them. She took notes on how they were organized and furnished and how the patients were treated and what they were fed.

By the time Florence returned home, she was an expert on hospitals and how they should be run.

Florence's parents were still very opposed to her nursing in a hospital in London, however. In those days, when well-to-do people were sick they were cared for in their own homes. Only the poor went to hospitals. Mrs. Nightingale could not bear the idea of her daughter working among such people.

"I absolutely refuse," she said flatly every time Florence returned to the subject. "A girl of your upbringing does not do that sort of thing."

"Anyway, your aunt is ill," she added. "Since you are so keen to nurse, I suggest you go and nurse her."

Florence did not like upsetting her parents, so she went to nurse her aunt.

"I am certainly happy to do what I can for Aunt," she confided to Lucy, "but I feel there are people out there who need me far more."

Her little friend understood how Florence felt. "Give it some time," she said. "Maybe your parents will change their minds." Lucy knew this was unlikely, but she wanted to keep Florence's spirits up.

Then, a short time later, something happened that allowed Florence to take things into her own hands.

Can you guess what it was?

Florence was offered a job! She was asked to take over as superintendent of a small London hospital. It was a special hospital for sick women of good background who had no families to care for them. Florence's task would be to completely re-organize it in new quarters.

"There will be a great deal to do, Lucy," said Florence.

"I know," replied Lucy, "but you will love doing it."

Once again Lucy was right. Florence threw herself into the job. She organized beds, carpets, curtains, pots and pans.

"The most important thing is that the hospital be clean and comfortable for the patients and that they feel loved and cared for," said Florence.

Her biggest problem was finding good nurses. There did not seem to be any who were properly trained. So Florence undertook to train them herself. She set strict rules and sent away anyone who would not follow them. At the same time, she showed the same compassion for her nurses as she did for her patients. She listened to their problems and saw to it that they were well and fairly treated. They responded by doing their work well and cheerfully.

Soon Florence had the best-run hospital in England. People began coming to study her methods of nursing, sanitation and hospital organization.

"Ah, Lucy," said Florence joyfully, "at last I am doing what I want."

About a year after Florence started nursing in London, Britain became involved in a war against Russia. Turkey, Britain and France wanted to stop Russia from taking some land belonging to Turkey. This land was called the Crimea. The British fought some terrible battles there against the Russians. Many men were killed and many more were wounded.

Soon the London newspapers were full of stories about the terrible conditions wounded and sick soldiers in the Crimea were suffering. The public began to demand that something be done to get proper care for these brave men.

"Reports from the battlefront are dreadful, Florence," said Mr. Sidney Herbert. "Men are dying by the hundreds from lack of proper food, clothing and medical care."

Mr. Herbert was Secretary of War and one of Florence's oldest friends.

"Something has to be done," he added, showing her sketches that had been made of hospital conditions. Florence was horrified when she saw them.

"I know I am asking a lot, Florence, but I want you to get together a group of nurses and go out to the Crimea and organize proper care for the sick and wounded."

Needless to say, Florence agreed to go.

Florence knew this was not going to be easy but she welcomed the challenge. "Come on Lucy, we have a lot to do and the sooner we are on our way, the better," she said briskly.

Florence immediately set about organizing what they needed for the journey.

"Our biggest task is finding competent and compassionate nurses to come with us."

"There aren't too many of those around," remarked Lucy.

Eventually Florence managed to recruit thirty-eight nurses, some of them nuns. Together they set out for the long journey to the Crimea.

At last, Florence and the nurses arrived at the British
hospital in Scutari. They were shocked at what they saw.

"Oh Ma'am, look at what they call a hospital!" cried one of
the nurses. "They don't even have proper wards. The men
are just lying in the corridors." They were long, windy old
corridors with rats running everywhere. There was no
running water and no heat. Rain leaked through the roof.

The Crimea, where the actual war was taking place, was across the Black Sea from Scutari. The conditions under which the British soldiers were fighting there could hardly have been worse. There were very few supplies. When winter came, it was bitterly cold. The men did not have enough blankets or food. They were fighting without coats or boots in freezing weather. Many were dying from exhaustion. Those who survived were very weak.

The wounded arriving by the hundreds at Scutari had been further weakened by the rough boat trip across the Black Sea. When they were left at the hospital, there was nowhere to put them except on the floor. There were not enough doctors to take care of them all, and many died before anybody got around to attending them.

In spite of the desperate shortage of staff, the doctors and officials did not trust Florence and would not listen to her. They did not like the idea of women in army hospitals, and they refused to let Florence or her nurses help with the wounded.

"What are we going to do Miss Nightingale?" asked one of the nurses. "We can't just stand around and watch these poor men suffer."

"Nor will we," replied Florence firmly. "For the moment there is nothing we can do about the men's wounds, but there is certainly something we can do about this place."

"Come on ladies, let's get to work."

And work they did. They scrubbed floors. They collected
straw and made beds for the sick and wounded. They rolled
bandages and made splints and set up their own kitchen
where they prepared the kind of food sick men could digest.

Still the doctors refused to let Florence's nurses tend the
wounded—until one day five hundred unexpected casualties
arrived at once.

"You must let us help you with the men," Florence urged
the doctors.

Reluctantly they agreed, and they quickly realized that
Florence knew what she was doing. They came to rely more
and more on her, and soon she was organizing the whole
place. She made changes in the kitchens, arranged for better
sanitation and more efficient distribution of supplies. But
above all Florence saw to it that the men were properly
looked after: they were washed and given clean clothes and
their injuries were taken care of.

Every night Florence would walk through the wards with her lamp.

"Come over and talk with me," one soldier after another would cry as she passed by.

Florence had a word for all of them. For the first time, the soldiers felt taken care of. They looked forward to seeing her quietly checking out her patients. They called her "the lady with the lamp."

Several times newspaper reporters stopped at Scutari on their way to or from the Crimean front. One was a very famous journalist called William Howard Russell from the London *Times*.

"Conditions are not good, Miss Nightingale," he said.

"I know," replied Florence, "but my nurses and I are doing the best we can."

"You seem to be the only ones who are. The other hospitals I have seen are far, far worse."

William Howard Russell reported back to London on the dreadful conditions in the army hospitals. He also told how Florence Nightingale was the only one doing something about it. As a result of his stories, Florence was soon famous throughout England.

"Lucy," Florence said to her friend one day. "I keep hearing about hospitals where conditions are even worse than here. I think I should travel around and see them. There may be something I can do." Lucy agreed. "Your nurses are so well trained they can look after things here for a while."

So Florence crossed the sea to the Crimea. The conditions in hospitals were indeed very bad. She gave advice on how things could be improved, but before she could see the work through something very sad happened.

Suddenly, Florence fell dangerously ill.

"I don't think she is going to live," said one doctor.

"We just can't let her die," replied another. "What are we going to do without her?"

When the men in the hospitals heard of Florence's illness they were very upset. They had come to love this beautiful, compassionate lady. As the news spread, British soldiers everywhere prayed for her recovery.

"Come on, Florence," whispered Lucy, "you must get well. So many people need you."

But poor Florence was so sick she could hardly hear her friend.

For many days Florence hovered on the edge of death. But her will to live was very strong. Finally the fever broke and slowly she began to recover. Everybody was very happy when she was well again.

As soon as she was strong enough Florence was back at work. She supervised the hospital and did her rounds, making sure that the soldiers were as comfortable as possible. She had her nurses write letters home for them and provided books and newspapers to help distract them. She made sure that their uniforms and nightshirts were clean and that their wounds were properly taken care of.

Before the war was over, many men owed their lives to Florence's care and compassion.

Finally, the war came to an end. But Florence's work was not finished. On the boat back to England she took care of the wounded.

"Florence, you must get some rest," said Lucy, alarmed at how thin and pale Florence was.

"Once I get home I will rest," replied Florence. "These men still need to be cared for."

Many people in England wanted to give Florence a hero's welcome, but she would not hear of it.

"All I want to do is get home to Lea Hurst and my family," she told Lucy.

When Florence arrived at Lea Hurst, her parents were shocked at the change in her.

"You are so thin," cried her mother. "You look so weak and tired."

"I'll sit in the sunshine and rest," said Florence.

After a few days Florence felt much better. Soon she was fretting to get back to her work. There was still so much to be done.

Artists had painted many pictures of Florence making her rounds with her lamp, and sculptors had made statues of her. When she returned to London, she was amazed to discover that people recognized her wherever she went.

"Miss Nightingale, this is my little daughter," women would say. "I have named her after you."

Everybody was talking about the wonderfully compassionate lady who had taken care of their soldiers in the war.

Another surprise was waiting for Florence.

A fund had been set up in her honor. Many of the soldiers she had nursed contributed to it. This fund eventually amounted to a great deal of money.

Florence was ecstatic. "Now I can open a real school of nursing, Lucy," she said. "A school where young girls can be taught about sanitation and trained in proper nursing methods."

She decided to set up the Nightingale Training School at St. Thomas's Hospital in London. St. Thomas's is still one of the most famous nursing schools in England today.

Queen Victoria of England had heard so much about Florence that she wanted to meet her.

"Miss Nightingale, it is an honor to meet such a compassionate person," said the Queen. "You have done wonderful work."

"Thank you, your Majesty," replied Florence, "but there is so much more we need to do. I am sure you agree that the health of your army is very important."

Queen Victoria did indeed agree.

"Yet even in peacetime," Florence continued, "the death rate among soldiers is higher than the general population's. That must change."

"I will  help you in any way I can," promised the Queen.

Florence worked very hard. She collected mountains of
information on the conditions in which soldiers lived. She
wrote hundreds of letters and spent hours and hours talking
to officials.

"Oh Lucy, sometimes I get so tired," she said, "I can hardly
stand up."

"I'm afraid your illness in the Crimea has had a lasting
effect on your health," said her friend.

Sadly, Lucy was right again. Soon Florence had to spend
most of her time lying down. But this did not stop her. She
simply did her work from her bed.

After many years of hard work Florence saw great results. Army barracks were less crowded, better ventilated and provided with reading rooms, and the men were better fed. The health of the soldiers improved. In India, where the death rate among British soldiers was particularly high, Florence suggested improvements in sanitation. Soon the death rate dropped.

It was now considered respectable for young girls to do nursing. Hospitals became clean and cheerful places and

people got better more quickly. Many nurses trained in the "Nightingale method," went abroad and worked in hospitals. They were always very welcome because of their superior nursing skills and compassion.

Even though Florence was an invalid for many years, she always kept in touch with her nurses. Florence was 90 when she died. The whole world mourned this extraordinary, compassionate woman.

Through her caring and compassion, Florence Nightingale changed a great many lives. Ordinary soldiers were treated decently and lived longer, healthier lives; hospitals were no longer places one went to die, but to get better; nursing became the honored profession that it is today—all thanks to that beautiful "lady with the lamp."

*The End*

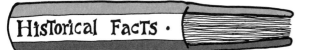

Florence Nightingale was born on May 12, 1820 in Florence, Italy, and was named after the city of her birth. Soon afterwards, her wealthy British parents returned to England, where she was brought up in great luxury.

By the time she reached the age of 12, Florence had become aware of the misery in which many less fortunate people lived, and had come to feel that the luxury surrounding her was wrong. At age 17, she wrote in her private notes that she had heard the voice of God calling her to service. Florence did not immediately know what type of service she was meant for, however. Only after seven years of uncertainty and frustration did it become clear to her that she was called on to nurse the sick.

So strong was Florence's calling that she refused repeated offers of marriage from Richard Monckton Milnes, later Lord Houghton, even though she loved him very much. She felt that her vocation demanded a life without marriage.

Florence Nightingale's family bitterly opposed her decision to nurse; hospitals in those days were mostly filthy places and nurses were often immoral and drunk. Florence spent seven more miserable and frustrated years unable to achieve her goal. These years were not wasted, however. Florence exchanged information with hospital authorities all over Europe and gradually became an expert on hospital administration.

In 1851, Florence's family relented and she was allowed to go to Kaiserswerth, Germany to gain nursing experience. Then in 1853, she was asked to take charge of a small London hospital. Florence accepted enthusiastically and set about completely reorganizing the Institute for the Care of Sick Gentlewomen in Distressed Circumstances. (It was later renamed the Florence Nightingale Hospital for Gentlewomen.) Her successful work at the hospital brought her recognition and respect.

In 1854, the Crimean war broke out. Reports from the front told of the terrible state of British army hospitals in the Crimea. Sydney Herbert, the secretary of war for the British government, asked Florence to lead a party of nurses to the war area. She agreed, and on October 21, 1854, she set out with 38 nurses. Upon their arrival at Scutari, Turkey, they found over 5000 wounded and sick soldiers, filthy and ill-cared for in huge dilapidated buildings which lacked even beds, mattresses and bandages.

At first Florence's efforts to nurse the soldiers were shunned by jealous army officials and medical staff, but she eventually won their respect. She established schedules for nursing care, kitchen work and diets, wrote countless letters demanding supplies and personally inspected every ward each day, sometimes working twenty hours without a break.

Then misfortune struck: while on a visit to the front lines, Florence Nightingale became dangerously ill

## FLORENCE NIGHTINGALE
### 1820–1910

with Crimean fever and almost died. She was urged to return to England to regain her strength but stubbornly refused so that she could continue her work. Her successful efforts to improve hospital conditions became widely recognized and she was given charge of all the army hospitals in the Crimea.

On her return to England in 1856, Florence Nightingale was hailed as a heroine for having saved countless lives through her revolutionary methods of hospital administration and nursing. But Florence did not consider her work finished, and she refused the honors and praise offered to her, fearing that popularity would create prejudice against her in the government. So completely did she disappear from public life that some thought she must have died.

Quietly, Florence Nightingale continued her work. Her concern now was with the living conditions in British army barracks. With the approval of Queen Victoria, she set about scientifically examining the health, diet and living quarters of British soldiers. In 1858, she published a huge book entitled *Notes on Matters Affecting the Health, Efficiency and Hospital Administration of the British Army*, which led to important reforms. She was called on for advice about sanitary conditions in the army in India, and about setting up military hospitals in the United States during the Civil War.

Not all of Florence's work related to the army. In 1860, she opened the Nightingale Training School for Nurses at St. Thomas's Hospital in London with funds that had been donated by the public in recognition of her work in the Crimea. The establishment of this school is now recognized as the beginning of modern nursing.

Overwork and the after-effects of her illness in the Crimea had by this time taken their toll on Florence's health. She became an invalid, and for the last forty years of her life, seldom left her room. For many of those years, she continued to work from her bed and was a hard taskmaster to others.

Her old age was tranquil, troubled only by the gradual loss of her sight. In 1907 she was awarded the Order of Merit, the first woman so honored. She died on August 13, 1910 at the age of 90.

# The ValueTale Series

| | |
|---|---|
| **THE VALUE OF BELIEVING IN YOURSELF** | The Story of Louis Pasteur |
| **THE VALUE OF DETERMINATION** | The Story of Helen Keller |
| **THE VALUE OF PATIENCE** | The Story of the Wright Brothers |
| **THE VALUE OF KINDNESS** | The Story of Elizabeth Fry |
| **THE VALUE OF HUMOR** | The Story of Will Rogers |
| **THE VALUE OF TRUTH AND TRUST** | The Story of Cochise |
| **THE VALUE OF CARING** | The Story of Eleanor Roosevelt |
| **THE VALUE OF COURAGE** | The Story of Jackie Robinson |
| **THE VALUE OF CURIOSITY** | The Story of Christopher Columbus |
| **THE VALUE OF RESPECT** | The Story of Abraham Lincoln |
| **THE VALUE OF IMAGINATION** | The Story of Charles Dickens |
| **THE VALUE OF FAIRNESS** | The Story of Nellie Bly |
| **THE VALUE OF SAVING** | The Story of Benjamin Franklin |
| **THE VALUE OF LEARNING** | The Story of Marie Curie |
| **THE VALUE OF SHARING** | The Story of the Mayo Brothers |
| **THE VALUE OF RESPONSIBILITY** | The Story of Ralph Bunche |
| **THE VALUE OF HONESTY** | The Story of Confucius |
| **THE VALUE OF GIVING** | The Story of Ludwig van Beethoven |
| **THE VALUE OF UNDERSTANDING** | The Story of Margaret Mead |
| **THE VALUE OF LOVE** | The Story of Johnny Appleseed |
| **THE VALUE OF FORESIGHT** | The Story of Thomas Jefferson |
| **THE VALUE OF HELPING** | The Story of Harriet Tubman |
| **THE VALUE OF DEDICATION** | The Story of Albert Schweitzer |
| **THE VALUE OF FRIENDSHIP** | The Story of Jane Addams |
| **THE VALUE OF FANTASY** | The Story of Hans Christian Andersen |
| **THE VALUE OF ADVENTURE** | The Story of Sacagawea |
| **THE VALUE OF CREATIVITY** | The Story of Thomas Edison |
| **THE VALUE OF FACING A CHALLENGE** | The Story of Terry Fox |
| **THE VALUE OF TENACITY** | The Story of Maurice Richard |
| **THE VALUE OF SELF-DISCIPLINE** | The Story of Alexander Graham Bell |
| **THE VALUE OF BOLDNESS** | The Story of Captain Cook |
| **THE VALUE OF COMPASSION** | The Story of Florence Nightingale |